HAWTHORNE

A collection of free verse and rhyme

Travis Martin

For Porter

peregrine

Like the deep, intimate thrum
Of the first phrasing
The beats of pulse, wings in wrest
Climbing to crescendo

A peregrine of verbiage in agress
Through cover of familiar diction
Devices amplify distress
Of her imminent strike

Complex, violently piercing lyricism
Punches through concentration
Piercing weak, inferior philosophies
The Poet feasts

residual

There's a kind of
Whisper
When the song ends

And your
Buds still hum
With resonance

And someone says
Your name
So you unplug them

Alone in a strange place
And you realize
Some divinity

alone

She felt she was wildly impervious to words
His were wiley and wit-fully immersive

Rushed to the finish to find
For one night only

He sweat, and swore
And struggled inside her

The clicks of heels and dreams
Splitting along her memories

Capitulation is the currency
Of the climb

coral

Her sanguine complexion
Strawberry speckled fae

Garnet red translucent satin
Beneath her alabaster skin

Jade toned rune stone emerald irises
Speckled rust and gold dust dynasties

Bangs of flames burning furious from winter
Lapping at heaven with calliope's fire

She hunts with a leopard's curiosity
Predatation of the spectacle

another relapse

The chill of spirit's pilot gasping
Foil tang of will collapsing

Happens swiftly
Sinking simply

Vivisecting facts of
Divergent motivations

Finding hidden entrances
Into ancient psychic prisons

What happens in sickness
Sticks through time

What's sick
Becomes the natural act

Of cogent
Self discovery

Be not beloved
Bite love

With toothy consonants and hard vowels

Be not love's derivative beloved

Be above it
Flower

going down

She touched his hand with furtive traction,
Her heels struck crisp; Six to four of his
Her hips swayed gently as
Stubborn was his swagger.

They passed by glances, looks that lingered
Glowering at each step toward the lift
Costumed bellboy with saccharin smiles
Doffed his cap opening the cage

Soft clacks of seven inch black
Patten leather cracked across marble
Tile like granite to steel
Till the elevator's scarlet carpet

He spoke awkwardly
Unsure, Inaudibly
Men explode at 'what'
For her life she'd be dulcet

devoured

Timid fingertips trespassing
Rowdy mahogany locks
Lips of hubba bubba
Breath escapes the ghost

To stand forever
At her doorstep
Never breathe air
That hasn't escaped her

Know only sensations
That pale in contrast
To the heat of her hips
And breast against mine

Amaretto and chorine
Consummated pheromones
Two decades past
And still ransom me

saunter

Excessive time in sorrow
Limbs always in sway
Dangling in silence
Save irregular

Tides of seizured steps
In the waning offset concrete sky of
Reflection of another autumn evening
Of the condemning men I was before

That I am inconsistent as
A cause, a kiss, a culture
Not at all what I was before
An offspring of man

flower

She'd walk the field of blooms
Plucking daisies and the daffodils
Resisting only the sunburst Dahlia

She grew, moved on, returning so often
To wander through Violas and the royal hyacinths
and visit her beloved Dahlia

One summer she returned with her daughter
Flowers in late bloom, "not the Dahlia darling
"You can pick the daisies and the daffodils."

"I can close my eyes and know it basks
Verdant as the first day that I found it,
I can know it is there, just like you're here"

"That's stupid, Mom. It's gonna die."
She kissed the girl and whispered
"Love is stupid. Stupid and beautiful."

king pen

She pursed her lips

In the bathroom mirror

Hunting creases in her smile

Before returning to the battle

hours pass

I discover the morning
Coffee brewed cold
Unfiltered and frustrated
Weeds fought the glade
For life
Magnolias limp atop their masts
Hours are after my advantages
Waiting below the window
Still
Compound derelictions
Establishing the timbre
Dense and incessant
Overtones of burnt umber

bar

He gave a dire glance
Hazily she cast it back
You know me, She asked
Not yet, He replied

Bold gold watch, power tie and ivory grin
Have you ever thought to model
Numb skin, Eyes just like the Salton Sea
Buy me a drink and who knows

She'd decided she deserved this
Face down on his acrid, sweat laden mattress
He cajoled himself and came on her thigh
because he fell out

She struggled as the asphalt
Swayed and drifted on the path home
Technicolor images of violations endured
Ran vibrantly surreal

corporal

Blue, wet clay eyes
My lens settled into
His cold head corridor
Decaying silence

Scent of spoiled blood
Is stickier in daylight
Until the night is on me
Thoughts that plot against

They come so genuine
Moonlight plays across the grey
Face peering from the wall locker
Hanging, when he's come

pyramid

Digging jagged strides
From dagger foiled footsteps

Chavez and Alameda
Dead rigs and asphalt

Alleyways and desolation
At the edge of incandescence

Texting something…
… succumb to a concrete stoop

Too far down Division
With a warm double India Pale Ale

Devour the world
as will an infant

Alarmed and awed
At every instant

Quelled and quieted
by the tenderness

Of a lullaby
And a kiss

embers

Scorched remains smolder from our
Battles waged on sovereign ground
Founded on a tryst that still bleeds
Cabernet and Bourbon

Faults that I confess
I've harbored
Long
Before I honored trust

Mornings you would rouse me
With radiant eyes
Rivaling the warmth and
Glory of the sunrise

Mornings you left crisply
Steely arguments quelled
Piloting compromise
Through ironclad mouths

such

Such a heavy head to carry
Over-filled with ideation

So I drag it on the asphalt
Refuse assistance cause it's noble

I can hear the cell doors clamor
Those great mechanical jaws

Around complacent shadows
Gnashing bones

hummingbird

I watch that listless Hummingbird
Whipping rigorous staccato
Suspended in space
As time escapes

Burning her elixer quickly as it enters
Deep desperate drag of life after another
No dwelling, as to idle is to die
Only the next delicious bloom

Pause for one deep inhalation
And one resolute sigh
And bask in the swiftly immediate life
Of the Calliope hummingbird in flight

hammer

Gingerly across this carpet
Stapled onto warped chip board

Old home, old bones
Paper thin walls

Tributaries of rust, like bolts of fire
Crawled across faulted chrome

Pop's ball-peen hammer
A strange iron diviner

My heart is less a part
Of this marriage
Than the magistrate

                              Maybe we should start with
                                   Getting that part
                                          straight

The wind song whispered

By the brown bone needles

Of the never fully failing

Evergreen

Two tweekers slap-sucking Jolly Ranchers
With moist salivic chops popping

Sharp crackling of tongues and lips
Flashing rot of mouth decay

Flipping through a white Prada clutch
Cautiously, meticulously sus

One more jackal-scan from the back of the bus
Discerning threats from hallucinations

Words Words
Nouns Verbs

Avoid alliteration in its
rhythmic iterations

Double entendre, like
Assonant consonants

Consonance for prosity of prose
Enjambment to force pause

black thumb

Crisp brown scales
cascade, clatter
Black thumb prevails

Lips touch down
Sweet. Sinister
deep, struggling breath

Icy winds
Rise whipping rabid
Settle and recess

Punch in
Log on
Check out

iPhone hum
Declares he has
not forgotten either

Sun is bold in
Buenos Aires!
Maybe next December

Corporate cutbacks
One more
cosmopolitan vacation

Window closing
Brats are only
anchors in this ocean

Narrow miss
Numbers improving
Classifieds postponed

Television on the fritz
endangering
existence

No more texts
Set up again
Fishing's getting slower

Need to get this right
A fern this time
Something not so thirsty

perseverance

The bricks lay woven
Struggling where seams bear crevasse
Where the weave dips deep

As the roots rise up
So gapes the groove
Independent earth

Nourished and persistent
Maturing curvature of
The gnarling terracotta weave

Respecting earth's dominion
To accentuate the aesthetic
Of the red brick patio

limbo

The crevasse between our glances
Our virulent transferences stretched
Across expanses
Of aeons and aeons.

Reactions to projections of herself
Unto me
Allegations of her infidelity
And ended just the way it would start.

A chapter of a love in limbo
Over
On a concrete bench
In Lower Lincoln Park

battles w/ bottles

One more tooth to gut
Collateral damage from
Time's staged offenses
Creases like crevasses

Slackened flesh, moisturized
Cold like granite fingertips
Hands that shiver and quake
As autumn leaves

A sense of self is still in hiding
Buried deep within my psyche
Like old bones in nightmares
Under the Mulberry tree

deeper still

Drank until her thoughts swam
Into riptides of sedation
And her head hung, 'hello'
She couldn't tell him no

With every new incision.
Deeper to the artery
Nearer to the indecision
Whether to try

Wet dreams of surrendering
In a creeping red erasure
Of venomous nectar
On toasted popcorn linoleum

Another week of empty doubles
Still she made the call for black
Figuring she'll pay him
With some indelible act

hipster

Jesus sandals with Velcro straps
And shorts made out of hemp

Button up free point collar shirt
An un-ironic recycling blue
DVDs in a sack

A Colorado creek ran through
His peppered ponytail
Tributaries of lost time

What's in the bag
I so nearly asked
I wanted to

As he walked past
He was transfixed by some
Electric dream

Strung by an idea or a face
Perhaps a moment in glass
Perhaps an IPA and mustache wax

You resonate beside me
A capture of nature
Wind through aspen leaves
Whispers from absentia

On the phone for hours
Till we slept, and some time in the night
I stirred to your soft saw on the line
Because we both refused surrender

And I woke to, Good morning
Yes, it is now, I sighed, And you
Only seven hours longer
I was so terrified you wouldn't show

The heat of your pulse
Throbbed in my palm
Pulling you into me
And we held on

infant

Three times they called me in
To shoot the child
Splayed out on the slab
"Abdominal compression,"

She recorded, and exhaling
Eight weeks old, smelled like nothing
Nothing like a twenty-some Marine
No black lungs or rotten adipose

Only a doll made of
Meat and bone
I tell myself tonight
But by then they've bled together

dwelling

Flames of minority rule
Lapping the Law like animals
With violent prosperity

        The heat of it
           Eats up
         The land

                And I stand in the pupil
                  Of another dilating
                      Mourning

amanda

Hair hung back like brown doll locks
Slack and slung like cheap yarn
One hand over her shoulder
One across her knees

A butt peaking from waxed lockes
Complexion tweaked in tattle
A rail waits at home
Scarecrow jeans, ratty worn

Stern gaze burning overspray
Until the bus bell rings
And she escapes
A stoned epiphany

my fiancé

Murders her days with lifted Prosecco
Corrosively gifted with lethal sensuality.

She claims her love with thick profanity
Tragic, fantastic, calamitous dynamo

Her tower constructed of unfettered vanity
Cast of skulls of foolish felled fellows

Waterworks bursting, performing excessively
Refusing to resign her old false woe

Yet affects a decadent ethereal tonality, (and)
Sachets a tongue of smoke across ground zero

To kiss my briar rose is falling into her gravity
She is tragic, O sweet calamity

handling

The easy path to
Evading defeat, protecting yourself
Escaping the snare of perilous accusations
: undefined/location_not_found

To grapple with gallium, galvanized
Twaddle and tattle, despicable cries
Pander to laughter with painful impressions
Feed her the muscle of malfeasant invention

Tell her what she wants to hear: device
Stupidly sputter your sodden confessions
Stutter opulently clear
So difficult to defeat escape velocity

The fiery lair of her Ire, smolders
Soul a stew, of fallow and sinew
Imploding in fission of
Violence and glycerine

Sara

She had fine sand hair
Like desert earth after the rain
Wild like a pixie thrush
Feral and beguiling

I buried myself into it
Bewitched with her scent
And held her for another hour

Our minutes showering
Into the abyss of one solitary night
As she and I dissolved
Into our alcohol solution

Pockets rumbling and drowning the pace
Of two inconstant and forbidden pulses
Until words began to burn
My tongue to turn them

And we held our eyes shut
Damning the brevity of night
Inhaling each other
Before we to our other lives

earnestly

She rises inside me like tides
And crashes against me
Like Gods against Exeter

Ever somber satisfier
Memories of morning kisses
Momentary recompense

She has always been there
Every avenue I wander
Though she promised nothing

Still, her sighs were dire
She would have me
Stir my fate for her

She'd guide me over nations
On the tight rope of a whisper
To defend her

tinder

She took me onboard
Into her vessel
Accepted me into
Her studio on Stark

The place in a bare
State of transition
I brought a six pack
She grabbed my sack

Daring eye to eye
'Do something'
And all was said and done
In thirty nine minutes

Our urgency dissipated
And passion disentangled
With formality I was thanked
While being ushered to the door

strung up

She's dangerous
Delicious
Hums with a din of bees
Walnut burle glassine irises

The permeating heat
Of those singularities
Tugging at my shadow self
Towards thorns of euphoria

at sea

Feel the sea quell
Far along the shore
Where beneath, the stars'
Reflections Clamor

Its swelling thirst
Swallows ships in gulps of
Men like flickering flames
These fragile candelabra

goose

She took me by my tie and said
I could hang you with this
We kissed

        She already had
        I confess

sparrow

My silly sparrow sang her song
I lied, it wasn't Love, but still I sang along
Her royal crest already molting
Never noticed this undress before

Her tang-dulcimer meringue melody
A song of monogamy turning me
I could not disguise my fallowing eyes
Her song lost its key. Hollowed the melody

The notes, the key, the tempo
Tonality disassembled
My fragile sparrow wailed
Until she struck the wall

Her final note reverberated
Turning to a fog
Heavy, cold, and residual

superfluous

This old Brain
Working against itself

Wit of jumping cholla
Fiercely unregulated

Flaccid wordage at the bar
Sanctimonious generosity

With a satchel full of
Five dollar adjectives

September

Such a wild child
That wails and quakes

As the crack of
Wind spun thunder
Rattles cheap windows
Threatening to break

Water creeping cross
The warped linoleum floor
Invading with
Monsoon currents

Collapsed skull
Where ceiling fell
Leaving gaping gore
Across the hall

Kelly's

More than a dollar
In the bar top quiz machine
Practically crackling
With anticipation

All quarters, and
The bar was clean as
False glass
Scant pour

The dense wood door
Swung open, bathing me
In the wet chill
Longing for me to inter

The second beer was full
From the second tender
And the third was on a hill
In the cold, quieting November

unexpected

The crescent moon perched
Like a wolfs tooth buried
In the great black paw

Chewing granola
Spilling her words abruptly
Causing a mess of curiosity

With a glance, a part
Of this open evening pageant
Invitation to ulterior motivations

mad party

The door drifts open
You are composed
A requiem written
In pheromones

You discover me
Standing like faith
At the cusp
Of a last stand

Phosphorus flame
Of your gaze, like a choir
Stirring my gait
Like a rounding Jaguar

Peripheral fixation
On each other's silhouettes
Immeasurable pressure
Against each other's chests

Sideways glances of
Deafening details
Two poised puppets
Anxious to entangle

Until my hot palm meets
The valley of your back
And you resist, inviting
Deeper contact

In the clamor of the patrons
Shifting tightly on the floor
Our heels, silent
Elevating our hunger

Your breath against my neck
With gossip all so decadent
Like a pulse of star-stuff
Through our arcing conduit

We sway like a buoy
On the dancing crystal surface
Of all these bodies churning, and we
Savoring each other like the sea breeze

The population recedes
Until there's only us
In electrical felicity

the wooden bucket

Morning's offense ascends and bites with shards
Through loose blade aluminum blinds
Wake in constricting fascia and slack skin.
Aching to drown in Tecate and Gin

Another call from the therapist
With messages of loosely intentional threats
Plastic amber bottles, empty as their glass compatriots
On a bed stand covered with dust and Advil PM boxes

Never a bar till four
Smokes and a guy off Prince for a dime score
Wife in a thread to the parents five days before
Still digging in my head from the iPad on the floor

Set fire to a lot last night
Like all that rattled on without a text riddled fist fight
Set fire to a lifetime of pandering
Finally conspired to demanding more than silence

Set fire to the uniform
Taking on a lover little more than a palindrome
Same way back and forward; Vacant forum
By nine I'm at the Bucket

shook up

She holds herself accountable
To things she says she's best at

Things she hasn't done yet;
Premeditated losses

She won't ask why
Holds her fingers in the flame

For the heat and for the pain
Nice to have him watching

Never wanted anything
Like just another hour to

Keep it going like this
Perfect like a picture

Framed under cracked glass
But won't ask herself why

first detour

I was absolute in my intention
To become a true dramatic artist
I still don't understand
Why I decided to enlist

The heat of gelled Fresnel lamps overhead
And the hush of captivated audiences
In uniform of camouflage
At every hour of the night

Strapped with my old issue Nikon
Searching for patterns
At the scenes of homicides
And so much domestic violence

In Marine Corps issue houses
I accepted I was lost.
And for a decade after discharge
I was listless

And the ill worded prose
Of Titus Andronicus
Became old wordy foes
Mocking my decisions

autumn

Bone thin dirty blonde
Shaking in the waiting room
Of a the 42nd street clinic
Living a hard twenty one

Raining down tears
Shitposting while bolstering
Inspirational memes
Between unsuccessful calls

To the child she'd already lost
Like prescriptions and her family's trust
Four administrative nurses
Debating which narcotic has her

Confidence in this system, gone
But her dealer lives on Hawthorne
Barely a mile away
Are easy solutions

about it

Wraith of a man weathered by
Raw wicked acts of trauma
Agelessly grizzled grilled by
Relentless defeat picked away at

Whispering mad, mad
Words into the
Realm he visualizes
Abandoned and unmedicated

A busted transient
On a metal bench
In the amber of a
Low light ordinance

'16

We spit love
That four letter word
Soft and deep
With hunger

I lose control
Capsized. I
Fuck my teeth chewing the diamonds
Of her eyes to dust

Remember when it felt good
Mad with the sickness
The ravenousness
Obsessed with penetration

Sweet stupidity
Damned lucid storming sensuality
Ruined us
By its eventual absence

pepper

Odd bars of melodic grace
Rich confusing grin crescendos
Blushing bouquets of Lavender hair

Eyes of oasis, shimmering
Ice in old growth forests
Cool hues and vivid wilderness

Without callous to cast off curiosity
Pepper sets fire to sorrow
That cerulean quickening

Sentiment the moment you look over
Separating weight from within
Casting spells against my viscera

Suddenly are reminded
Of abundant satisfaction
Deep in this scarlet stone

Without deviation from her
Fantastic succulent sonnet
Swiftly exquisite tragic liaison

empty vessel

There's a baby at the end of the hall
Slaughtering silence with wicked tremolo
Although our walls swallow treble
We are temporary vibrations

Farcical fathers gnash porcelain teeth
Beneath motionless white leather
Beady blue oculus guzzling Fox News
Imagining the world simply isn't organic

Grotto tiled in terracotta linoleum
Whitewashed walls reflect
Reverberating emptiness within
Without

dapper

This wet cigarette slides in beside me
On the #4 Division from Gresham
She entered the scene already rambling

A well dressed tower
Surrounded by five debutantes
Gracefully captivated by his vowels

She compliments his tattoo
It's a bible verse from Hebrews
she shares about her dream tattoo

A portrait of herself, nude in the dirt
dead, and I'm pretty sure she said
With a chair coming out of my eye

She sobs intermittently, vacillating control
Her boyfriend won't French kiss her anymore
She just hopes he's the big one

Because she's never ever really been in love
And then she loped from the bus
Nobody said a word but the Dapper Man

Then

You stood there
nearly weeping
Green serpents coiled

In the reservoirs of your eyes
And he stood there in concentration
Snake charming

untreated

Silently swallowing violence in
Her sweat soiled seat on the max
Murky smoke stained porthole eyes
Blackened teeth grind and crackle
A sweater held together by sheer will

She wags her face as she rocks and shakes
A shivering burlap bag on a branch
Muttering refusals like incantations
Cast deep within the illegible canto
Of her mistreated and unmedicated mind

sack

Thin lipped and unshaven
His Powell's sack
Swung with slack as he sauntered
With aimless trajectory

Eyes that scanned in a head
Set forward, in a way that said
I'm carefree and approachable
An unassuming antagonist

She weaves left, then right
For the door, with a wide birth
Many times, she's experienced
His variety before

fleeting

This opalescent sphere descended
Along a monsoon pour off creek
Shivering with intermittent raindrops

Stravinsky's Firebird suite escalated
The bubble itself suddenly burst
We're all that temporary

rehab

That same humming bird
Hovered. Fluttered
Isaiah took note

I smoked my illegal
Newport to the bone

Lenny in his lavender scrubs
I never saw him smoke
Though he'd bum them

Bacchus bounced around
On methadone

They upped his dose
Made everyone admire
And loathe him

Andre always appeared
The moment you started
To talk shit

the mother

S he paid for the daycare
So he wouldn't balk
About her poverty

It's been worse, has been her mantra
Ever since he served her papers
Aggressively pursuing custody

"You make our son kind"
Towing hope on a tight rope
Losing her fucking mind

I want somebody
to save my spirit
It scales our cathedral
Flesh peeled and blackened

I want a fighter
To make me brave
I want a lover
To inspire me

It raises its torn hands
To surrender its entirety
By the pageantry
It is smote

I want a girl like
Some for religion
I want a deity to
Desire my affection.

shitfaced

They trundled up the funny little stairs
Stumble mumble drunken pair

She giggled is he in there
Sssh come on he doesn't matter

Rumble fumble nearly there
They blundered up the funny stairs

killingsworth

The green line hauls ass
Stutters to pause at the platform
A cigarette butt climbs
Up the ramp to the front

Not without labor
Disguised as swag
Lugz and a black puff coat that shimmers
Like quilted obsidian

Face peppered indecisively with hair
Bulging eyeballs cruise the car while
Conspicuously sucking mike's hard lemonade
Cradled in his voluminous cellophane shell

haunted

Everyone was scared
Of the ghosts
In the old building
We chose to be
Sequestered in
For rehab
Again

We got the chance
To hunt around
In the night
With a staff liaison
All we did was
Use the opportunity
To fuck

i don't believe

I won't believe
n your surrender
nto anything arcane.

But how you draw
This river of mica
To the mouth
Of a thing serene.

After all that foments,
Calamity settles to your will
You're of a science undiscovered

monsoon

The Mother of Thousands'
Musty pheromone erupts
Engorging the atmosphere with it
And releasing into a desperate desert.

The Silver oxide sky
Surrenders to her kiss
A gash of light
Flashes silently

In famished moments
Thunder growls and moans
And by her command
Comes down hard and heavy

Undressed and owned
By the wild tempered
Punishment of a
Canyon monsoon

Sedona

The sun descends and pops
Upon deep jade thistles of
The palo verde's claws

Oxblood berries of
Juniper trees
That ape crooked as

The old drunk's ego
Nod to the black cherry
Valley of sand

Mystical vortexes
Whip up wild ions
As hawks soar low

For desert mice
That hide beneath that
Verdant prickly pear

leave me for your dirt

Sweet and salted
Early morning stillness
Deep inside
Her kiss

Her leg up against me
So warm and bristly
Like a jaguar's tongue

Her thigh against mine
Stoney and distant
Like the last bite

Somber tree-song
Mourning Autumn
Six feet deep within
Her kiss

inside

I see you there
nside my bones
Standing staring
Never alone

When I am dead
I will be sloughed off
Blood down the drain
Bone shards in the sewer

Still you are there
Set by the fire
Crackling scared
Body in cavernous

Moments, silently screaming
Still so aware, you were
Devils in lonesome despair
Cupid's pupae

Weep in dread, starved for kisses
Mothers in sentimental winter
Into the slots for rainbows
Last rains until cataclysm

hanging on

I wake on the sofa
Old friend

Arms across my chest
Like a last viewing

Head so heavy
Gluttonous gravity

Lead in all my capillaries
Frosted glass teeth

Cold viscous sweat
On my forehead and feet

Another day off
Finish my Bota Box

Of shit Chardonnay
Dawn barely cracking

Only a slew of novella length messages
From me in a drunken state

please

The sacred flame that gnashes
Bloodied on the fingertip

Of an afternoon encounter
Flickers

Trading in those decadent whispers
For dagger-tongued stabs

Run those icy fingertips up my thigh
Take me uninvited

Mutilate me with your excitation
Conjure me a divine horror

Breathe that exhaust of a billion of us
Choking on each other

seventh

I've seen you become
Vapid in elusive amber hues
Renown you slip away
Without a warning

I've watched you since you were
The sixteenth of December
Cold and bare and desperate
And confused

I've felt you come upon me
Like emotion and
Helpless to persuade you
To remain another day

His preference is for absence
She surfeits on duress

Though the children will diverge
And He shall clamor for his mettle

The heart degrades
Old silky words leave filthy residue

While she'll uncover attributes
He'll discover anonymity

Though both evolve
And both against the sea

On separate tides
To become their newest iterations

redeemed

Still stalking
Outside the wire,
Underneath my shadow
swallowing gravel

Imagining a forest fire
In the lungs of jurisprudence
Retracts
To somber observations

Of
The sinner
The redeemed
The righteous and the wicked.
The glorious hypocrites
With nefarious
Ideologies
Of

Nuclear reactors
Molecules in cataclysm
Atoms in chaotic rhythm
A show of farce

tiny deaths

There are no long halls
Or bright lights for tiny deaths

Only revelations in showers
Cold expressions at the end

Condemned exchanges
Play as the shower shatters

And you realize the cruelty of
Exactly what you said

And you meet
Another tiny death

definite

Her gaze is lead lined.
Straigning my ego's foundation

Her figure seems to bend space
Like a feline, or a flame

Splitting me apart in her clutches
Beautifully brutally, totally awesome

the performance

When the light descends
Where the clamor falls to murmured
Hushes in the tiers and rows
Anticipation like tsunami rising
The silence magnifying
Till super massive and crushing

Under the black cast till the curtain
Breaks tucked behind a fleet of artists
Curious to find how their canvas
Bears the strokes
Of their calculating expressions
Their conveyance and their voice
The tap reverberated with her step

In the silence
The felted night arena of
The poised theatre wept
Beneath the bold hued lights
Crackles the sizzling anticipation
Until her first phrasing ignites

common sense

When the dog bites the child
Put that fucker down.

The Human right
Our oath to death

We do our best impressions
Of discreetly cruel divinities

For humanity because we all plot fear
Humans are these oblivious seers

Fat free diet driven
Tanned tyrannical simian cattle

summertime

When summer gives its so oppressive grasp
And lets the bliss of moonlight overcast
The final act of the shadow marionettes
Tempts and taunts of fate and flesh and fucking

She, with delicate expressions and the
Toss of her eyes, and belayed confessions
Cannot be a part of what I'd prefer to be
Silently unencumbered by any interaction

My eyes, of late, toss disingenuous greetings
With so shallow as a furrowed brow flat effect
Eyes ahead, isolated, by the fear of failure
Morning comes redeeming opportunities

poets

We crush ideas,
And ferment thoughts,
To keep for dark occasions.

Stash them in cerebrums,
Mine, cultivate, and abuse them
And peddle them for approval

So lovers can intoxicate
Themselves upon our
Bitters.

mistakes

I loved her again at last
Against the Portland pewter canvas
I decried her doubtful platitudes
Resisting fears of love's collapse

Love is a scent to savor,
A secret sacrilegious flavor
A racing notion that hungers for
Constant thought and blind surrender

What I hoped would be my end of seeking
Was to her, a search for a means to an end
A dissipated scent, stagnant and faint
Devoid of ceremony

brea

A toy for her smile
Swooning momentarily
Swearing it was only she and I
In explosions of negative ions

O' to hear the chorus
Cast across her mind
How they sang her arias in
Quixotic herbal half tones

Eyes like walnut and ash
Thighs in diaphanous
Cotton which fell into them
With delicious eternity

'20

Winter rain gallops and trots
And shatters against the asphalt
Cracked and faulted
Like our democracy

This city blissfully inviting virulency
Meandering and shopping
Abusing and accosting
Caricatures of indulgence

Celebrations of capital
And silence to the solstice
Marks another revolution
Of the earth eater

Chandelier

Raindrops hang like
tea light sparks
at the tips of
leaf bare tendrils
of a winters Palo Verde

silently

*S*he sits upright in dark arrest
Inscrutable voices casting hexes
Showering malfeasance upon her
Like the rotting winter

Histories

Down these vacant halls we roam
Built of brick cement of bone
Lit with songs of old gods
Beckoning to the unborn

We haul all our lore
Our fantasies and rot
Discovering surrender is to
Sacrifice our delicate unknowns

Stranded

I long for the dark static
of your indecisive rains

For your urban scriptures
and post-modern glyphs

Your creators interwoven
like one mycelium mother

Birthing light and biting
cynicism of sprite wit

This place I'm stranded in
has an expiration.

Malingering Recruits Platoon (MRP)

I was flanked by my escort
To medical to assess my ankle
Fractured Fibula and a bum knee

In Medical Rehab Platoon
We traveled around in twos
Me at the time on crutches

I glimpsed this would-be
Marine drinking listerine
He stole from our witch docter